St Ælfheah (St from Deerhurst to Mai...y........ (.....): some Millennial Reflections on Religious Ideals

Nicholas Brooks with Alan Thacker

My first task is to explain how a Deerhurst Lecture on St Ælfheah comes to be given in April 2013, rather than in September, the traditional month for all previous Deerhurst Lectures. This lecture had, of course, originally been scheduled for September 2012, but at that time I proved to be prostrate in a hospital bed. My wife, Chloë, and I would like to take this opportunity to thank our chairman, Michael Hare, the chief organiser of the Deerhurst Lectures, for his practical, tactful and efficient support then, when my future was in the balance. We are also grateful for his (and his local team's) kind hospitality, which has ensured that today's arrangements here have worked so smoothly.

Moreover (as Michael has explained to you) this is actually the second Deerhurst Lecture to be devoted to the topic of St Ælfheah; that might indeed seem one too many. The first, entitled 'St Ælfheah: His Life and Cult' was given in September 1994 by Dr, now Professor, Alan Thacker, probably Britain's greatest expert on the cult of saints in the early Middle Ages, and indeed on the cult of English saints in particular. In 1994–5 Alan Thacker was in the throes of moving from the Liverpool base of the Victoria County History for Cheshire to London in order to become the Head of the whole 'VCH' organisation, and was taking on the massive administrative responsibility of persuading local authorities to support their local county VCH projects at a time of ever-growing pressures on local authority finances. Not surprisingly Alan's file with his Deerhurst Lecture got buried during that move and was indeed long deemed irrecoverable. Hence our Chairman's suggestion in Autumn 2009 that I might revisit the topic of Ælfheah, particularly in the light of my work on Canterbury Cathedral in the Anglo-Saxon period. Very recently Alan's 1994 Lecture, in its antiquated 'Wordstar' format and dot-matrix font, has indeed resurfaced and he has generously made it available to me. In consequence this lecture is very much a 'Brooks *and* Thacker' production, with many ideas and some of the wording deriving from Alan's original text. My task tonight has indeed been hugely facilitated by Alan's generosity in putting his text at my disposal and then by agreeing that the resulting publication in 2013 should bear both our names.

It has also proved possible to illustrate this published version (as with my actual lecture in April) with coloured representations of the *Life of St Ælfheah* from the stained glass of Canterbury Cathedral. I am hugely grateful here to Professor Simon Keynes, who had included these images in a lecture on

Archbishop Ælfheah that he delivered in Canterbury in September 2012 and to Michael Hare for facilitating their transmission and reproduction. Both have been very patient and tolerant of one who, in retirement, lacks the support of professional IT technicians and is uncomfortably close to being a technophobe. So this publication has been blessed with their generous assistance.

In order to understand St Ælfheah's career and martyrdom in its context, it is necessary to appreciate two crucial features of the political and ecclesiastical background to the lifetime of the saint. The first is that many of the English political difficulties of the 990s and 1000s derived from the fact that King Edgar had died young in 975, aged 32, and had left just two male heirs — Edward and Æthelred — both of them minors, being aged about 10 and 7 respectively, but also being the offspring of successive queens. Indeed Edgar's first wife seems to have died when giving birth to Edward, who had therefore had to be brought up by foster-parents. King Edgar had soon remarried, this time to Ælfthryth, daughter of Ordgar, the Ealdorman of Devon. It was in March 978 when the older son, the boy-king Edward, by then thirteen years old, was visiting the household of his young half-brother and of his stepmother Ælfthryth at Corfe in Dorset, that he was shamefully murdered. It is as a murdered prince that Edward is known to history as 'Edward the Martyr'; and his cult actually seems to have been encouraged by those surrounding the young Æthelred, in part perhaps as a means of deflecting suspicions of their direct responsibility for the murder.[1] The whole episode cast an inevitably murky shadow upon the long reign of the younger brother, Æthelred (978–1016).

Secondly the English episcopate in Ælfheah's day was dominated by men who had been trained as monks in the English monastic reformation of the second half of the tenth century. Successive archbishops of Canterbury – Sigeric (991–4), Ælfric (995–1005) and then Ælfheah himself (1006–12) – had all begun their ecclesiastical careers being trained in reformed Benedictine monasteries, as indeed had most of the English bishops appointed between the 960s and 1010s. Belief in the power of communal worship was fundamental to such men, belief that communal prayer would mitigate God's evident anger at the sins of the English. His anger was surely manifested in his punishment of the English with renewed pagan Viking raiding.

St Ælfheah's career, as recorded a generation or so after the Norman Conquest,[2] begins with his abandonment of his paternal inheritance when he was professed as a monk here at Deerhurst, perhaps in the early or mid-960s. He is said to have subsequently established himself as a hermit at Bath; one would love to know where in that borough among the ruins of its Roman baths and buildings his 'hermitage' had been situated. The hermit Ælfheah then attracted followers there before becoming their abbot in that city. Later, in the year 984 he was appointed to succeed St Æthelwold as bishop of Winchester.[3] We learn nothing of Ælfheah's parents, nor indeed of the location of their home, which might have been quite close to this beautiful church. But in the 960s there were several other reformed monasteries or minsters in Gloucestershire or Worcestershire where the young Ælfheah could have been sent for his initial education.

Next I should like to clear up a basic point of pronunciation and spelling; for you will find many variations on Ælfheah's name in available works of reference and even more in popular publications, historical, ecclesiastical and antiquarian. The spelling that I have used [Ælfheah] and which was used in all the publicity for this lecture might be classed as the normal spelling of the name in classical (West Saxon) Old English of the late tenth and early eleventh century, that is in 'standard Old English'. In the course of the eleventh and twelfth centuries, however, a great variety of spellings can be shown to have actually been current in different texts, Latin and English, from different areas and contexts. Ælfheah, Ælfeagus, Alfheh, Alfy, Elphege, and Elphegus are the most commonly found forms, but more variants could be cited from contemporary or nearly contemporary sources. The actual pronunciation of the name, however, seems to have varied much less than did the spelling, and we should note that spellings beginning with *E*- and containing -*ph*- in place of -*f*- seem either to postdate the Norman Conquest or to be the work of Continental scribes at work in England during the reign of Edward the Confessor (1042–66).

So at last we come to our main topic tonight, that is to the career of St Ælfheah and to ideas aroused by consideration of his career, first as a Benedictine monk and hermit, then successively as abbot, bishop and archbishop during the middle years of the reign of King Æthelred II ('the Unready'; 978–1016), when the Viking threat to the English political and religious establishment proved to be at its height. It is, however, a sad reflection upon the memorialisation of English saints in the years after Ælfheah's martyrdom on 19 April 1012 that no *Vita* or *Passio* was produced at Canterbury, at a time when monks who had known him there were still alive. It is, of course, not unusual for our knowledge of the details of the life and career of an early medieval individual to lack the basic biographical facts on which a secure chronological reconstruction needs to be based. What we are told of St Ælfheah in later accounts therefore lacks the authority that might be attributed to the memory of contemporaries. Instead it derives from the writings of Osbern, who was indeed one of the most talented English monks whom Lanfranc found at Canterbury when he came there as archbishop in 1070. However, Osbern was also one of the most difficult members of the English community, being virulently hostile to Norman rule; he had soon to be sent away to the great Norman abbey of Bec to learn monastic obedience under the aegis of Abbot Anselm. He was later to return to Canterbury, apparently now accepting his new Norman lords, but nevertheless determined to record and glorify the Old English past of his community.[4] His writings were therefore responses to the general inadequacy in the documentation of English saints that Lanfranc and the Norman monks whom he introduced to Canterbury found; only St Dunstan had been memorialised (not entirely adequately) before the Conquest.[5] Osbern's *Vita Elphegi*, written with Lanfranc's encouragement at some date between *c.* 1075 and 1089, was in fact the first work of the extensive programme of local hagiography produced at Canterbury in the generations after the Conquest.[6]

There are, perhaps, some faint hints in Osbern's work that some traditions had been accurately passed down within the Christ Church community from Ælfheah's days, alongside (it must be admitted) some inaccurate details. Though Osbern seems to have known little or nothing of the circumstances of Ælfheah's election to the archbishopric, he does tell a curious story of his journey 'across the Alps' to receive the *pallium* from the Pope (who can be identified as John XVIII, whose pontificate lasted from 1004 to 1009). He recounts how *en route* when at the vill of Ausonia, Ælfheah had been attacked by the inhabitants and robbed of all his moneys, but had continued on his way; whereupon the inhabitants found their houses ablaze until they restored all the treasures to the archbishop elect, who promptly forgave them and thus caused the blaze to dissipate.[7] Yet *Ausonia* is Auxonne-sur-Saône, which would indeed be an unlikely stage in any transalpine journey to Rome. If there is a Canterbury memory underlying this story, it would seem clear that Ælfheah had in fact been avoiding the dangerous crossing of the Alps, where half a century earlier Archbishop-elect Ælfsige had met his death in the winter of 958–9.[8] Ælfheah must instead have been skirting the Alps and taking the longer, but safer route down the Saône and the Rhône to Marseilles. Osbern preserved the name of the town where Ælfheah had been attacked, but (perhaps fortunately) did not have the geographical knowledge of the routes to Rome to understand the implication of his journeying via Auxonne.

Next I want to emphasize tonight that our understanding of Viking activities in King Æthelred's reign derives very largely from the year-by-year record of events found in different manuscripts of the *Old English Royal Annals* (formerly and probably still to most historians today) known as the *Anglo-Saxon Chronicle*.[9] The seven extant manuscripts of this work are conveniently known by the letters A–G; and their different provenances and the different dates of their script have occasioned much learned debate, which need not concern us here. What we do need to know is that the 'A' manuscript (the earliest that survives) was being kept and occasionally updated at Winchester, in the Cathedral community of the so-called 'Old Minster' there; whereas the 'C', 'D' and 'E' manuscripts (written in widely separate houses) all share essentially the same account. I have suggested (in an interpretation that seems to hold the field currently) that the version that lies behind the C, D and E manuscripts had been disseminated intermittently from the household of the king, and that its account of Æthelred's reign was produced in the year 1022 (the sixth year of Cnut's reign), but drew upon material that had already been recorded annually by priests in Æthelred's service. We should also notice that these annals normally use the Old English word *fyrd* for English armies but choose a different word, *here*, for the ravaging Viking forces; once, however, in CDE's annal for 1006 the English army itself did so much damage that the annalist used the term *inn here* ('home host') for the English army and *uthere* ('foreign host') for the Viking force. Such language has biblical resonances, which I have endeavoured to preserve by using 'army' to translate the English *fyrd* but 'host' for the Viking *here*. It is also necessary to warn that although these annals are our earliest sources for the events of Ælfheah's capture and martyrdom and though they have an apparent concentration on 'facts', they are not necessarily more trustworthy than later sources; each annalist may indeed have had his own agenda.

What emerges very clearly from the different manuscripts of the annals, especially when combined with information from Welsh and Irish annals, and what seems indeed to have eluded historians until Professor Keynes' detailed reconsideration of the evidence is that the character of the renewed Viking raiding on the British Isles changed very clearly in the year from 990 to 991.[10] In 980, 981, 982, 987, 988 and 989 there had indeed been short-term raids, conducted during the Summer and Autumn by Viking armies from various Scandinavian settlements that then took back to their homes whatever booty they had managed to seize before the onset of Winter. But the host that defeated the East Saxon forces under Ealdorman Byrhtnoth in the battle of Maldon on 10 or 11 August 991 had – either by design or in response to its victory – in fact stayed campaigning in Britain for several years thereafter. A very similar pattern of short-term raiding being replaced by raiding hosts that remained many years in the West has indeed long been detected by historians investigating the development of Viking activities in the ninth century.[11] Moreover Archbishop Sigeric's counselling that a huge tribute of £10,000 should be paid after the disastrous defeat at Maldon suggests that he may have been aware that the danger then being faced was of a new order of magnitude, because that host was not intending to return home that Autumn.[12]

When we move on to look at the shared account in the CDE annals of the capture of Ælfheah during the sack of Canterbury in 1011 and then of his martyrdom in 1012, we need to keep in mind that this account was disseminated in 1022, that is whilst the body was still at St Paul's, London, a full year before it was to be ceremoniously transferred to Canterbury. Already in 1022 we can see in the *Royal Annals'* wording some hints of conspiracies: the host had got into Canterbury through the treachery of one Ælfmær, whose life Archbishop Ælfheah had saved, and … a little later … the host *allows* Abbot Ælfmær (of St Augustine's) to escape when they carry the archbishop off with them to Greenwich. There, when Ælfheah had been pelted with 'stones, bones and ox-heads' (presumably the debris from food-preparation in the host's camp) one of the members of the host struck the archbishop down with an axe; the very next day the burgesses of London and Bishops Eadnoth (Lincoln) and Ælfhun (London) had received the martyr's corpse and buried it at St Paul's, where St Ælfheah's power was already (i.e. by 1022) being revealed by miraculous signs. Thus the *Royal Annals* here provide evidence for the early development of the cult of Ælfheah within London and for the value that was attached to possession of his relics there.

5

Next we need to consider a contemporary continental source, namely the *Chronicle* written in Saxony between 1016 and 1018 by Bishop Thietmar of Merseburg (who died in 1018). Merseburg, situated on the river Saale (just south of the modern Thuringian town of Halle), had in Thietmar's time long served as a frontier town on the German/Slav border. Thietmar may actually be our earliest source for Ælfheah's martyrdom (though I prefer to consider the *Old English Royal Annals* as effectively a strictly contemporary annual record, even though filtered through a lens of the year 1022). Moreover, Thietmar was writing some 400 miles (640 km) away from the martyrdom-site at Greenwich. His German (or rather 'Saxon') readers might be expected to feel some common identity with the Anglo-Saxon peoples in Britain, but had no experience of their spelling or pronunciation of names. Thietmar's account is therefore full of errors in the recorded names of participants and places, and may serve as a splendid example of how quickly errors could occur in details that had been recently conveyed by oral tradition. Thietmar claims on the authority of a certain Sewald that 'a perfidious force of Northmen, led by Thorkel, had taken captive the noble prelate of the city of Canterbury, called Dunstan(!), along with others whom they had ill-treated with chains and hunger and indescribable torments after their abominable custom'.[13] The archbishop (Dunstan) is reported as initially promising them money with a fixed term for its payment; but when the term was up, his claim of dire poverty makes him seem a liar to the Northmen. He offered his body in recompense, but Thorkel *dux* intervened, offering to pay the money, so long as they no longer sin against the Lord's anointed and on condition that he could keep one of the ships for his own use. The anger of his colleagues was not softened by Thorkel's intervention and they let loose a stream of ox-heads, stones and blocks of wood. One colleague was indeed crippled as he attacked and so had cause to realise he had sinned against Christ's elect. Thietmar quotes Romans xii. 19: 'Vengeance is mine saith the Lord, and I will repay' and notes that these Northmen had indeed both lost God and the money offered to them; whereas for Thietmar Christian sinners had by constant prayers now acquired a powerful intercessor (Dunstan or correctly Ælfheah) whom they believe to have 'much power with the Divine Majesty'.

It is, I think, reasonable to suppose that Thietmar had some access, whether directly or more probably indirectly, to the account in the *Old English Royal Annals* of the events of 1011 and 1012, that is of the capture and martyrdom of Ælfheah. But in that process all Old English names of persons and places, and even the identity of the archbishop involved had become hopelessly confused or mangled. Subsequently in the later eleventh or early twelfth century elaborations of the life of Ælfheah appear in England. John of Worcester following, I believe, a lost Canterbury Chronicle, identifies the ransom demanded for the archbishop as £3,000, a sum which fits well with the additional sums paid for other notable prisoners in this era.[14] John also names the man who slew the saint as a certain Thrum (whose rare name arouses curiosity since it appears to be the dative of an Old English word *thruh*, literally meaning 'trough', 'coffin' or

Plate 1
The legend of St Ælfheah in a window at Canterbury Cathedral (North Choir Aisle IX).
By permission of the Dean & Chapter of Canterbury.

Plate 2
The siege of Canterbury by the Vikings (from the St Ælfheah window at Canterbury Cathedral). By permission of the Dean & Chapter of Canterbury.

Plate 3
Archbishop Ælfheah is taken in captivity to a Viking ship (from the St Ælfheah window at Canterbury Cathedral). By permission of the Dean & Chapter of Canterbury.

Plate 4
The martyrdom of St Ælfheah or The massacre of the monks and citizens of Canterbury
by the Danes, heavily restored (from the St Ælfheah window at Canterbury Cathedral).
By permission of the Dean & Chapter of Canterbury.

'tomb'). John claims that Ælfheah had actually confirmed Thrum as a Christian in an adult baptism just on the previous day. Most historians today, I suspect, would be more inclined to conclude that such accounts reflect improvements in tales that were being told and retold in monastic communities to validate the power of local shrines. It would be dangerous to presume that they establish the persistence of accurate tradition within those communities, except where (as with the name of Auxonne) they record circumstantial detail.

Osbern's later work on Ælfheah's *Translation* to the cathedral church at Canterbury is structured to facilitate specified readings for the Octaves (i.e. the weeks succeeding) of the martyrdom and the Translation of the body to Canterbury. Notice first of all that – following an Anglo-Saxon tradition perhaps deriving from Bede's *Ecclesiastical History of the English People* – Osbern was very precise about the dates of the martyrdom in this booklet on the *Translation*: in 1012 between the evening of the Saturday of Easter week and the beginning of Sunday Ælfheah received the crown of martyrdom in the seventh year of his archiepiscopate and the fifty-ninth of his life.[15] Osbern therefore reckoned that Ælfheah had been born in 953–4 and had succeeded at Canterbury in 1006. He asserts that the transfer of Ælfheah's body to St Paul's had been made 'either freely or for a price' (*siue gratia seu precio*), which we may choose to regard as a Canterbury writer's slur on London's claim to the martyr's body. He has, however, to admit that miraculous cures had already taken place at the site of the tomb at St Paul's, but gives only the vaguest account of them. He was much more concerned to tell in detail the wretched ends that met all those who had participated in slaying the martyr. Moreover, in the *Translatio*, Osbern claims that the sufferings of the English army at the hands of the Scandinavian host had actually been prophesied to them by Ælfheah and even more remarkably that the Christian King Cnut had been advised that Ælfheah's burial at Canterbury, where he had wished to lie, would best ensure the end of any pagan Viking threat. Finally Osbern reported the miraculous opening of the seemingly impenetrable tomb at St Paul's. His account rests on the authority of two named Christ Church monks: *Godric*, who had been a pupil of Ælfheah and was later dean of the pre-Conquest community (*c.* 1052–70) and *Ælfweard the Tall*, who had been in the household of St Dunstan, and thus was associated with Christ Church's other major pre-Conquest archiepiscopal saint. Whatever one may make of Osbern's claim that many yoked pairs of oxen could never have pulled the stone slabs of the tomb apart, thus establishing that its opening was indeed miraculous, there seems every reason to accept that Godric and Ælfweard were real pre-Conquest monks of the Cathedral community, who were indeed responsible for the initial (oral) dissemination of an account of the translation. We should be cautious before following those historians inclined to accept details from the account in the *Old English Royal Annals* (which had to be acceptable in the royal household in 1022) in preference to this Christ Church story. Differing views are likely to have developed among English and Norman monks in different houses at various times in the eleventh century.

Some fifty years later when William of Malmesbury was compiling his 'Deeds of the Bishops of England' (*Gesta Pontificum Angliae*) between 1125 and 1140, having first undertaken an elaborate programme of visits to all the main churches of England and to their archives, the stories around the martyrdom had become ever more elaborate. William provides intriguing stories of the drunken night-time carousing that had developed among those attracted to Ælfheah's following at Bath, until the ringleader was struck dead by God; and Ælfheah is said to have (fore)seen two devils beating his protesting corpse. When the archbishop informed the guilty ones next day, they promptly (William tells us) adopted temperance! William had similarly little specific information about Ælfheah's activities as bishop of Winchester, but that does not prevent him waxing lyrical on his abstemious diet (avoiding meat save when ill) and on his ascetic regime of night-time immersion in the waters (presumably in one of the streams of the river Itchen, where indeed Wykehamists bathe to this day). When elected to succeed to the archbishopric, he retells Osbern's story of his journey to Rome to receive the *pallium* and being beset by thieves in a hamlet (*vicus*) when crossing the Alps and the miraculous outbreak of fire in the thieves' houses and its abatement when they returned the treasures. Finally when the archbishop was a captive of the Viking host, William has stories of how the Viking host was beset by illness or plague (*tabes*) which killed many quickly and painlessly until Ælfheah gave communion to those who had caught the infection and miraculously cured them. William also recounts that after the martyrdom the saint's body remained incorrupt and his blood still fresh, such that an apparently dead branch (*lignum*) which had lost all its bark, when smeared with that blood, was found next morning to be revived, in flower and with incipient fruits! William claimed that the body still remained incorrupt and the blood still fresh, when the tomb had been recently re-opened; indeed he excuses himself from wearying the reader with yet further stories of the disastrous ends that met all the saint's killers.

What should we make of these stories as told by William of Malmesbury (as indeed of those recounted earlier by Osbern)? They had been told to William by devout monks and abbots in the course of his tour of English religious houses. Though his own skill as an author may have led him to improve their telling by clothing them in particularly lively language, there is no reason to think that he was himself inventing these stories. Yet the studied vagueness of the stories as to the participants, the locations or the occasions suggests that the tellers did not share our perception that any supposed 'fact' needs to be backed by a calendar-date and an AD year for it to be held to be credible. The trustworthiness and authority of the teller was much more important to William. It is rather to anthropologists' accounts of the development of oral history in settled communities to which we should turn in an attempt to assess such 'memories' and tales. Stories develop in such communities, precisely in order to serve current needs of those communities. It is no surprise therefore that William's stories of Ælfheah should reflect the values and imperatives of early twelfth-century monasticism.[16] We should of course not presume that *we* today are in any way immune from similar pressures, for just in the last fortnight we have experienced very different 'takes' attached to the life of the late Margaret Thatcher. They have all too obviously been presented to us with the current needs of particular local regions and of particular political parties in mind.

Finally we come to the coloured illustrations (Plates 1–4) which are drawn from the late twelfth-century stained glass windows from the north choir aisle of Canterbury Cathedral. They illustrate scenes from Osbern's *Vita Sancti Elphegi* and show that that author's work did succeed in inspiring his successors in the cathedral community to take pride in their English identity later in the century, when the linguistic divisions had become less polarized and less politically sensitive. We see first of all (Plate 1) the overall window depicting in three roundels separate scenes from the *Life of St Ælfheah* (window IX of the North Choir aisle of Canterbury Cathedral). The stone tracery of this window dates from the romanesque building work of Prior Conrad (1107–26), but the window-glass was installed under William of Sens, after the disastrous fire in the Choir of 1174 had destroyed whatever romanesque glazing there may once have been.[17] We can examine in turn each of the three roundels. They depict firstly (Plate 2) the siege of Canterbury by the Viking host; notice that the artist has depicted both the Viking attackers and the burgess defenders wearing mail armour (hauberks) and helmets with nasals, in other words they are shown in contemporary twelfth-century armour. Next (Plate 3) we see the captured Archbishop Ælfheah being taken onto a Viking ship, whether at Canterbury or perhaps downstream at Fordwich or in the Wantsum; and finally (Plate 4) we seem to have the martyrdom of St Ælfheah, shown on the left, and with Thrum wielding his axe, just alongside to the right. The right-hand half of this much-restored roundel has been interpreted in its present form as showing the slaying of monks and burgesses of Canterbury, but unless a whole further window is missing from the scheme, it would seem more likely that it actually depicts the slaying of those who had participated in the martyring of St Ælfheah, as Osbern describes.

Conclusion

We must in conclusion openly admit that the extant sources do not allow us to create a convincing biography of Archbishop Ælfheah; those sources are local hand-written accounts intended for the most part to be read just by the members of particular monasteries; they were not 'published' or printed with the intention that they should be pored over by modern historians with all the advantages of editions with parallel translations and comprehensive indexes. But these sources do nonetheless show us different interpretations of Ælfheah's life, which itself had been spent in a variety of institutions. Most of those whose views survive today were monks in English Benedictine communities, but one was a German bishop of a Thuringian frontier city, and some were probably chaplains in the English royal household at an early stage of their own careers; one was a brilliant craftsman-artist (and may perhaps even have been a layman) in the cathedral workshop at Canterbury. I hope that I have convinced you that a thousand years after the killing of Archbishop Ælfheah in 1012 there is still much fascination in investigating their different interpretations of that traumatic event.

NOTES

[1] Modern understanding of the murder of Edward derives from the discussion in D.J.V. Fisher, 'The anti-monastic reaction in the reign of Edward the Martyr', *Cambridge Historical Journal*, 10 (1950–2), pp. 254–70 and S.D. Keynes, *The Diplomas of Æthelred the Unready 978–1016* (Cambridge, 1980), pp. 163–74, which can be supplemented by C.E. Fell, 'Edward King and Martyr and the Anglo-Saxon hagiographic tradition', in *Ethelred the Unready*, ed. D. Hill, British Archaeological Reports, Brit. ser. 59 (1978), pp. 1–13 and S.J. Ridyard, *The Royal Saints of Anglo-Saxon England: a Study of West Saxon and East Anglian Cults* (Cambridge, 1988), pp. 140–75.

[2] For the relevant works of Osbern of Canterbury, John of Worcester and William of Malmesbury, see below, nn. 3, 6 and 15.

[3] *Chronicle of John of Worcester*, s.a. 984, ed. R.R. Darlington and P. McGurk, II (Oxford, 1995), p. 434, who was followed by William of Malmesbury, *Gesta Pontificum Anglorum*, ii. 76. 1–9, ed. M. Winterbottom, I (Oxford, 2007), pp. 258–70. At the Old Minster Ælfheah was remembered as responsible for the marvellous new organ and for moving the tomb of St Æthelwold to the choir of the enlarged cathedral; see Wulfstan of Winchester, *Life of St Æthelwold*, ed. M. Lapidge and M. Winterbottom (Oxford, 1991), pp. xxx, 66.

[4] A. Gransden, *Historical Writing in England c. 550 to c. 1307* (London, 1974), pp. 127–8; R.W. Southern, *Saint Anselm and his Biographer* (Cambridge, 1966), pp. 248–52.

[5] *The Early Lives of St Dunstan*, ed. and trans. M. Winterbottom and M. Lapidge (Oxford, 2011), pp. lxiv–cxxxiv; M. Lapidge, 'B and the *Vita Dunstani*', in *St Dunstan: his Life, Times and Cult*, ed. N. Ramsay, M. Sparks and T. Tatton-Brown (Woodbridge, 1992), pp. 247–59; A.T. Thacker, 'Cults at Canterbury: relics and reform under Dunstan and his successors', *op. cit.*, ed. Ramsay, Sparks and Tatton-Brown, pp. 221–45, at 222–4.

[6] Osbern, *De Vita et Passione S. Elphegi*, in *Anglia Sacra*, ed. H. Wharton (London, 1691), ii, 122–42 (for a translation, see F. Shaw, *Osbern's Life of Alfege* (London, 1999)); cf. Eadmer, *Vita Anselmi*, I. xxx, ed. R. Southern (Edinburgh, 1962), pp. 50–4 for an account of Anselm's learned judgment that Ælfheah had indeed shown the qualities of a martyr (despite differing circumstances) and his acceptance at Bec of Osbern's assertion that Ælfheah had been martyred for attempting to convert his pagan captors.

[7] Osbern, *Vita S. Elphegi*, ed. Wharton, ii, p. 129 (trans. Shaw, *Alfege*, pp. 45–6).

[8] Ælfsige's fate soon influenced Canterbury views of the *pallium*-journey to Rome. Dunstan was hailed after his return from Rome in 958 as *Tu astutus colober, cervus qui transilit Alpes* ('Thou clever snake, thou stag who bounds over the Alps'), see W. Stubbs, *Memorials of St Dunstan*, Rolls Series 63 (London, 1874), *Reliquiae*, no. X, p. 371. This is a double-edged joke, since Professor Lapidge draws to my attention that *astutus coluber* is used in patristic sources for the devil; see Gregory, *Moralia in Iob*, xvii. 32 and Bede, *In prouerbia Salomonis*, iii. 3.

[9] For the suggestion that our understanding of the genesis of the 'Chronicle' is in need of major revision, see N.P. Brooks, 'Why is the *Anglo-Saxon Chronicle* about kings?',

Anglo-Saxon England, 39 (2011), pp. 43–70; id., "Anglo-Saxon Chronicle(s)' or 'Old English Royal Annals'?', in *Gender and Historiography: Studies in the Earlier Middle Ages in Honour of Pauline Stafford*, ed. J.L. Nelson, S. Reynolds and S.M. Johns (London, 2012), pp. 35–48.

[10] The best interpretation of the developing nature of Viking activities at this time remains that of S.D. Keynes, 'The Historical Context of the Battle of Maldon', in *The Battle of Maldon AD 991*, ed. D. Scragg (Oxford, 1991), pp. 81–113, with his elucidation of the complexities of the command of the 991 army at pp. 88–90.

[11] N.P. Brooks, 'England in the ninth century: the crucible of defeat', *Transactions of the Royal Historical Society*, 5th ser. 29 (1979), pp. 1–20; reprinted in my *Communities and Warfare 700–1400* (London, 2000), 48–68.

[12] *Anglo-Saxon Chronicle CDE, s.a.* 991.

[13] *Die Chronik des Bischofs Thietmar von Merseburg*, VII. 36–43, ed. R. Holtzmann, MGH, *Scriptores rer. Germ.*, n.s. ix (Berlin, 1935), pp. 448–51 (trans. D.A. Warner, *Ottonian Germany: The* Chronicon *of Thietmar of Merseburg* (Manchester, 2001), pp. 332–7).

[14] See S.D. Keynes, 'The historical background', in *Battle of Maldon*, ed. Scragg, p. 100.

[15] Osbern, *Translatio S. Ælfegi*, ed. and trans. A. Rumble and R. Morris, 'Textual Appendix', in A. Rumble, *The Reign of Cnut* (London, 1994), pp. 294–315, at 294–5.

[16] C.H. Lawrence, *Medieval Monasticism* (London, 1989), pp. 156–71, 193–7. For introductions to the huge scholarly literature on oral tradition, see J.M. Vansina, *Oral Tradition as History* (London, 1985); *The African Past Speaks*, ed. J.C. Miller (London, 1980); and J.W. Fentress and C.J. Wickham, *Social Memory* (Oxford, 1992).

[17] M. Gibson, 'Normans and Angevins 1070–1220', in *History of Canterbury Cathedral*, ed. P. Collinson, N. Ramsay and M. Sparks (Oxford, 1995), pp. 38–68, at 53 and 64; *The Windows of Christ Church Cathedral Canterbury*, ed. M.H. Caviness, Corpus Vitrearum Medii Aevi, Great Britain, II (Oxford, 1981), pp. 70–1 and (black and white) plates 53–4; and for the coloured plates see M.A. Michael, *Stained Glass of Canterbury Cathedral* (London, 2004), a work unavailable to me in Birmingham.